a season of sundays 2004

Images of the 2004 Gaelic Games year by the *Sportsfile* team of

photographers, with text by Tom Humphries

An official GAA publication, published by Sportsfile

A Slice of Life...

Cork and Kilkenny parade before the All-Ireland Hurling Final, 2004.

You only make it to the All-Ireland Final through hard work, dedication and the endless pursuit of perfection. These basic values are the foundation of any team's quest for the highest quality standards. This applies as much to the business world as to the sporting arena. At Carroll Cuisine we follow these same values in the preparation of quality food for your enjoyment.

As gaelic games are an integral part of sporting and social life, so Carroll Cuisine is truly a part of daily life.

The Slice of Life!

Fond memories of special moments

Carroll Cuisine is very proud to be associated, once again with *A Season of Sundays,* this superb pictorial record of the 2004 season of Gaelic Games.

The dedication and commitment of all those associated with our games during the year is brilliantly captured by the outstanding team of photographers at Sportsfile.

JOHN CARROLL
MANAGING DIRECTOR
CARROLL CUISINE

The games, which occupy a special place in our lives, continue to amaze us with the levels of performance and achievement rising every year. The determination to succeed, together with the extraordinary output of passion displayed every week, provide us with a truly unique sporting canvas and in 2004 left us with some very special memories.

The intensity of competition saw levels of fitness, discipline and work ethic, reach new heights and the marrying of the traditional values of the games with a "professional" approach in terms of training, development and preparation, made for some remarkable performances on the fields of play this year.

The year in question was also a remarkable one for Carroll Cuisine. The integration of our business into the IAWS Group was a very positive development, enabling us to take a significant step forward in our business development. As part of the IAWS Group, we have retained and are building upon our traditional values, built up over almost 30 years as a family run organisation. We are also spreading our wings by investing in a new manufacturing facility which enables us to explore new ranges of products and services for our customers.

As in our national games, we have a firm belief that values still have a very strong place in today's highly competitive world, be it in business or sport. We are delighted to continue our commitment to our games through our sponsorship of the Offaly county teams and through this very special reflection of the sporting year.

We hope that *A Season of Sundays* will provide you with recollections and fond memories of the many special, and sometimes emotional, moments which are captured so well in the pages which follow.

A Season of Sundays is now in its eighth year. It has become part of the annual reflection of not just our sporting year in Gaelic Games but the way of life we cherish throughout the country.

Enjoy.

All the colour, passion, excitement and intensity of Gaelic Games

Is chúis mór áthas dom an deis seo a fháil cúpla focail a scríobh ar fhoilsiú an leabhar seo.

It is a sure sign that the GAA season has come to a close when one's mind begins to turn to the latest installment in Ray McManus' pictorial account of Gaelic Games and its associated affairs, *A Season of Sundays*. Incredibly, this is the eighth year that this colourful and vivid account of the passion, excitement and intensity of Gaelic Games has been produced and it has quickly become a must have for all GAA fans.

This year's championship provided many highlights, including, in football, the provincial championship breakthrough of Westmeath, the epic journey that was Fermanagh's march to the All-Ireland semi-final and those great Munster and Leinster final victories for Waterford and Wexford in hurling. At the end of the day, it was the old reliables of Corcaigh in hurling and Ciarraí in football that were to bring home the bacon. The glory, the pain, the tension and wonder of those great games are all captured in magnificent detail by Ray and his Sportsfile team.

Yet, the GAA season is about so much more than those great days in the sun. It is about the chilled hope offered by the O'Byrne Cup or the FBD League; it's about those lonesome days in the wind and rain at dark venues in the National League; it's about the passion and intensity of the struggle and the pride of parish and place that defines the club championships. It's about the players, the managers, the supporters, the families, the great goals, the forgotten points, the gatemen, the programme sellers, the marching bands, the hats, the flags and the headbands. It's about everything and everyone that marks us apart and it is all captured so wonderfully and so memorably within these pages.

I want to pay tribute to Ray and the entire Sportsfile team for their dedication to the coverage of Gaelic Games over the years. We see them in the sunshine of Phoenix or Rome, in Sydney or Paris covering the All-Stars, the International Rules or the Interprovincial championships. More importantly, we see them hunched to the wind and soaked to the skin in the rain of Carrick-on-Shannon and Ballybofey or frozen to the bone as the O'Byrne Cup stutters to life in Aughrim, Drogheda or Tullamore.

They bring to life the GAA season and make Monday mornings an easier place to be.

Ráth Dé oraibh go léir.

Seán O Ceallaigh

SEÁN O CEALLAIGH
UACHTARÁN
CUMANN LÚTHCLEAS GAEL

The Sportsfile team

Matt Browne   Brendan Moran   David Maher

Text

Tom Humphries, The Irish Times

Statistics

Séan Creedon

Co-ordinator

John Mahon

Design

The Design Gang, Tralee

Colour reproduction

Mark McGrath

ISBN: 0-9523551-8-3

Published by

SPORTSFILE

Patterson House, 14 South Circular Road,

Portobello, Dublin 8, Ireland

www.sportsfile.com

Photographs

Sportsfile staff portraits on location at Croke Park by kind permission of Cumann Lúthchleas Gael and Páirc an Chrócaigh Teoranta

| Damien Eagers | Pat Murphy | Brian Lawless | Ray McManus |

New angles, new faces, new stories

Every summer is different and has it's own personality. Every game is different too, but within those summers and those matches, the choreography of games is often similar. Two trained hurlers chasing a sliotar will often look like any other pair of hurlers chasing a sliotar. Two men competing to haul down a high ball will look like any other two men doing the same. A *Season of Sundays* looks for the differences which make every summer unique.

When we assemble this book every autumn, the pictures we look for aren't just the ones which provide a faithful record of what happened, we look for the shots which make a difference, which give a feel for the summer just past. A moment. A score. A celebration.

Every year we end up with a collection of new angles and new faces and new stories. The shots mark the joy of arrival and sometimes, as this spring, they mark the pain of a passing.

This year's *Season of Sundays,* as always, is a collective effort and with that in mind I would like to thank my colleagues at Sportsfile for their skill and enthusiasm and Tom Humphries for his wonderful prose. I would also like to thank you, the readers, for supporting us down through the years and trust that you will find this latest installment a fitting tribute to the players, spectators, and officials who make our national games the wonderful institution that they are.

Ray McManus

Beyond that dressingroom door, there is victory and heartbreak, pain and pleasure, noise, crowds, loneliness, shouts, speeches, hugs, tears, setbacks, breakthroughs, injuries, argument, flags, desperation, optimism, hope…

Carlow 2-09 Wicklow 0-12   O'Byrne Cup

Early doors. Cold weather. Hard work. The footballers of Carlow make their way onto the pitch at Dr Cullen Park before their O'Byrne Cup game with Wicklow. The game will stretch to extra-time and a three point win for the home team

"I have the Westmeath manager's shirt on me, that's who I am for the moment… for two years." …Páidí Ó Sé.

Muhammad comes to the mountain. And he carries his own bags… for now

Backbencher. An Taoiseach, Bertie Ahern, TD, watches the annual Dublin Blue Stars fixture between the Dublin footballers and the Dublin Blue Stars Selection from the rear of the crowd at Naomh Mearnóg, Portmarnock, Co. Dublin

O'Byrne Cup   **Carlow 2-08 Dublin 0-13**

A nice cup of Lyons tea. Before the Dublin v Carlow game in the O'Byrne Cup in
Dr Cullen Park, the Dublin manager Tommy Lyons pours forth for the final time
before a season long silence. Selector Dave Billings eyes the biscuits

Happy days. Carlow's year gets better and
better and it's only January. Carlow's physio'
Eddie Jackman embraces manager Mick
Condon at the end of the game

All good things… Carlow's O'Byrne Cup run came to an end on the day that Westmeath gave the first intimations of their worth. Rory O'Connell and David O'Shaughnessy, the Westmeath midfield, do battle with John Hayden and David Byrne of Carlow in the semi-final of the O'Byrne Cup, played at Cusack Park in Mullingar

Years ago in Dublin, there were faithful men who stood in solemn committee sessions behind the goals at club games and acted
as umpires and mentors and advisors and hecklers. They were known as blackcoats and you don't see them anymore.
At Tailteann Park in Navan though, like an apparition with his back to the stone, a man removes his cap and stands straight for
the national anthem. Did he ever stand behind a goal in Sillogue or St Anne's or Ringsend Park?

Back to the scoring board. In Scottsdale, Arizona, Pat Smith, from the host club Phoenix Gaels, is kept busy as he marks up the 11th goal for the 2002 All-Star team. The game finished 11:20 to 13:10 in favour of the 2002 All Stars. Neither goalkeeper was available for comment afterwards

The prize of winter. Westmeath had the O'Byrne Cup final in their own back garden in Mullingar. A record attendance of 14,612 showed up and got nothing but the same old story. Meath by a point

New Boss. Same old hoodoo. Páidí Ó Sé, left, studies the ground as Sean Boylan watches the play in the O'Byrne Cup final at Cusack Park in Mullingar

First blood: Ray Magee, captain of Meath, lifts the O'Byrne Cup after victory over Westmeath

Early in the National Football League game between Longford and Kerry in Pearse Park, there was a rainstorm. Glistening spectators withdrew to the shadows. Outside, more of the rain fell on Kerry. Longford scored a goal after thirty seconds. Tom O'Sullivan was carded. Longford scored another goal in injury time. Just enough to beat Kerry for the first time in thirty one years. For Kerry, and their new manager Jack O'Connor, September in Croke Park seemed many light years away

Meath's rollercoaster year really got going in February at Navan. Hosts to Galway, they obligingly fell behind by 1-6 to no score after just fifteen minutes. Then they reverted to Meath ways and Meath laws. Darren Fay, all at sea in midfield, resumed his tenure at full-back. Meath kept believing and chiselled out another one of their against all odds victories

Big day, small crowd. Only 1,800 people turned up in the Gaelic Grounds in Limerick to see their county
footballers play their first ever game in the top flight of the National Football League. Those who stayed
away lost out. Stephen Kelly of Limerick, in the centre, tussling with Tom Kelly of Laois, scorched the earth
with his pace, scored 1-2 of his side's total and contributed handsomely to an eleven point win

When Kerry looked back on their season from the vantage point of their All-Ireland win, they pointed to a night under floodlights in Tralee as being the moment when they began to galvanise. Faced with their old rivals and neighbours from Cork, they scored nine points in a sparkling second half to win by just two points. Here, Willie Kirby and Eoin Brosnan show Dermot Hurley of Cork just what they have learned about the art of defence by playing Ulster teams for the past couple of years

As good as it gets, for today anyway. Longford travelled to Cusack Park in Mullingar for a game between the dark horses of the league. They duly beat Westmeath with a contribution of 1-2 apiece from the Barden brothers, Paul and David. Here, David exults in his goal. Later, he will be dismissed for a second yellow card

A journey of a thousand miles begins with one small step. Mayo, unheralded
and unrated back in February, prepare to emerge into the light for their
League game against Dublin in McHale Park, Castlebar

Cormac McAnallen. There is little left to be said or written about his short life or glorious times. One Sunday afternoon in February, he was leading out his beloved Tyrone side in front of 10,000 applauding spectators in Pearse Park, Longford. The following weekend, he was lifting the McKenna Cup. The weekend after that, he was playing in a challenge for Eglish against Cullaville. Then, he was gone. The space he left behind will never quite be filled

Everyone say "cheese." Local photographer Mike Shaughnessy arranges the Galway hurlers in
presentable order for the team photograph before their Allianz League game against Kilkenny.
Understandably, the players have other things on their mind

Somebody told Pa Buckley to get that face checked. And he did! War paint in order, Pa watches the League game between Limerick and Tipperary at the Gaelic Grounds in Limerick. The hat is just for good wear

A bruised sky, and the flag at half mast against it, as the death of Cormac McAnallen is mourned throughout the nation. Black armbands, solemn silences and welling grief mark the passing of a beloved son of the game

Tyrone retired Cormac McAnallen's number three jersey for the
year. As the Tyrone players huddle before their League game
with Mayo in Castebar, Ciaran Gourley, chosen at full-back,
wears a jersey with the number 31 on it's back

From the stands, Brendan and Bridget McAnallen,
parents of Cormac, watch the game unfold

Growing up wearing the colours of Newtownshandrum, John McCarthy
never won a medal. He could just see retirement coming when a wave of
young talent swept into the club's senior team. In March, at the age of
32, McCarthy played in the AIB All-Ireland Club final as captain of the
club he loves. Here, he chases down Gregory O'Kane of Dunloy

AIB All-Ireland Club Hurling Championship Final   **Newtownshandrum 0-17 Dunloy 1-06**

Dunloy have been here so often before, listening to winners' speeches and graciously suffering the cursory three cheers for the losers. Paddy Richmond is comforted by Chris Morrisey, a lifelong member of Newtownshandrum, in a little cameo of what the club game is all about

And after. Back in the club's traditional jersey, John McCarthy lifts the Andy Merrigan Cup, watched by GAA president Sean Kelly and Donal Forde, Managing Director of AIB

Shouts in lilting gaelic echoing around Croke Park, great tribes of brothers and cousins
playing for either side, teams of friends hailing from small parishes which literally empty
behind them when they travel to Croke Park. Caltra, a team drawn from just twenty houses
in Galway, play An Ghaeltacht from Kerry, in the most resonant of All-Ireland Club Finals.
Aodhán MacGearailt of An Ghaeltacht is tackled here by Jarlath Murray of Caltra

Noel Meehan, captain of Caltra, lifts the
Tommy Moore Cup after Caltra's win

Allianz National Hurling League   **Clare 1-12 Kilkenny 2-10**

Ground control. DJ Carey keeps his nose after the sliotar as one, two, three, four Clare defenders bear down on him, literally. Brian Lohan and Brian Quinn lead the posse in the National League game at Cusack Park, Ennis

Football, a glove story. Seamus O'Neill and Karol Mannion of Roscommon in action against Ciarán McManus of Offaly in the Allianz League game at Tullamore

Cork travelled to Healy Park in Omagh needing to beat Tyrone in order to have a chance at progressing in the League. On a day when the home side suddenly looked fatigued and ordinary, Cork couldn't take advantage. Fionán Murray's last minute miss in a drawn game summed up Cork's afternoon of frustration

When Tipperary play Cork, it's always carnival time. Hence the amount of customers on the terrace (one) beats the amount of customers on the ferris wheel (zero). The game ended in a draw

Déjà vu. A Kerry man encrusted in Tyrone men. In Healy Park, Omagh, Johnny Crowley
attempts to free himself from the octopus that is the Tyrone defence unit composed of
Ciaran Gourley, 31, Ryan McMenamin, 2, Brian Dooher and others

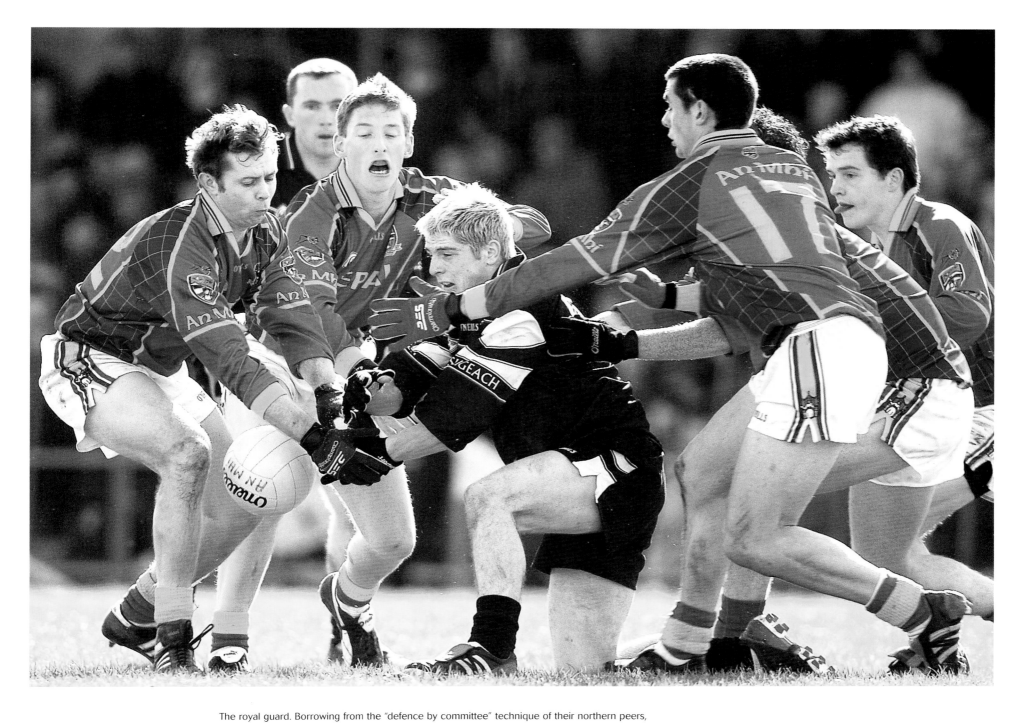

The royal guard. Borrowing from the "defence by committee" technique of their northern peers,
Meathmen Cormac Murphy, Trevor Giles, Tomás Comer, Anthony Moyles and Seamus Kenny
swamp Brian Curran of Sligo in the National League game in Markievicz Park, Sligo

The embrace of spring. Former soccer player Eoin Keating gets
his weight behind a tackle on Armagh's Justin McNulty

Limerick's promise appears to be blossoming. Mike O'Brien,
right, celebrates with Stephen Lucey following their side's
victory over Armagh in the Gaelic Grounds

Like conjoined twins shadowing each other's moves, David Collins of Galway and Tom Kenny
of Cork do battle in the Allianz National League game at Pearse Stadium in Galway

The ever innovative Mark Foley of Limerick tries his new boomerang tackle
on Alan Kerins of Galway in the League game at Pearse Stadium

Spring time produces a couple of unlikely classics. Tyrone and Galway need two games to separate them in the National League semi-final. In the second game, played at Pearse Stadium in Galway, the home side go eight points up early in the second half before Tyrone come storming back into the game. Galway might have been spared the agonies associated with a two point win had Derek Savage slotted this penalty home. Instead, it flew tamely towards the chest of Pascal McConnell in the Tyrone goal

Carlsberg don't do Masses, but if they did… The women of the Ladies Football All-Star team get Mass in the bar of Fitzpatrick's Hotel on Lexington Avenue in Manhattan. Fr. Liam Kelleher, the National PRO for Ladies Football, does the things that other PRO's can't do and celebrates the sacrament before the All-Stars versus Rest Of Ireland game at Gaelic Park

A Bronx tale. Gary Ruane of Mayo is tackled by New York's Eric Bradley in the Bank of Ireland Connacht Senior Football championship game in Gaelic Park

On the end of a twenty six point defeat and exiled in New York. There have been better days

Tug of war. Colm Quinn of Offaly yanks the jersey of Down's
Michael Higgins during the National League Division 2 final

Ciarán McManus, captain of Offaly,
is congratulated by the faithful

"You wouldn't have to be a rocket scientist to figure out that the last few years haven't been great for Kerry teams coming up here." Seamus Moynihan

Kerry came to the Allianz National Football League final in May with a point to prove to themselves. They hadn't reached a League final for seven years and all recent trips to Croke Park had ended in misery. On a Sunday in May they turned a corner. Eoin Brosnan soars with Galway's Joe Bergin

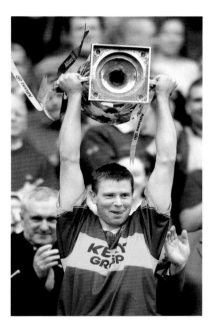

Kerry captain Tomás Ó Sé lifts the trophy to mark Kerry's seventeenth National League win

Nobody knows you when you're down and out. Westmeath captain
Darren McCormack wears the jersey of his teams conquerors as he
sits on the turf in the Gaelic Grounds in Limerick and takes in his
sides Division 2 Hurling League final loss to Down

Meanwhile Down captain Simon Wilson begins
the celebrations by lifting the trophy in the
company of Allianz Chief Executive Brendan
Murphy and GAA President Sean Kelly

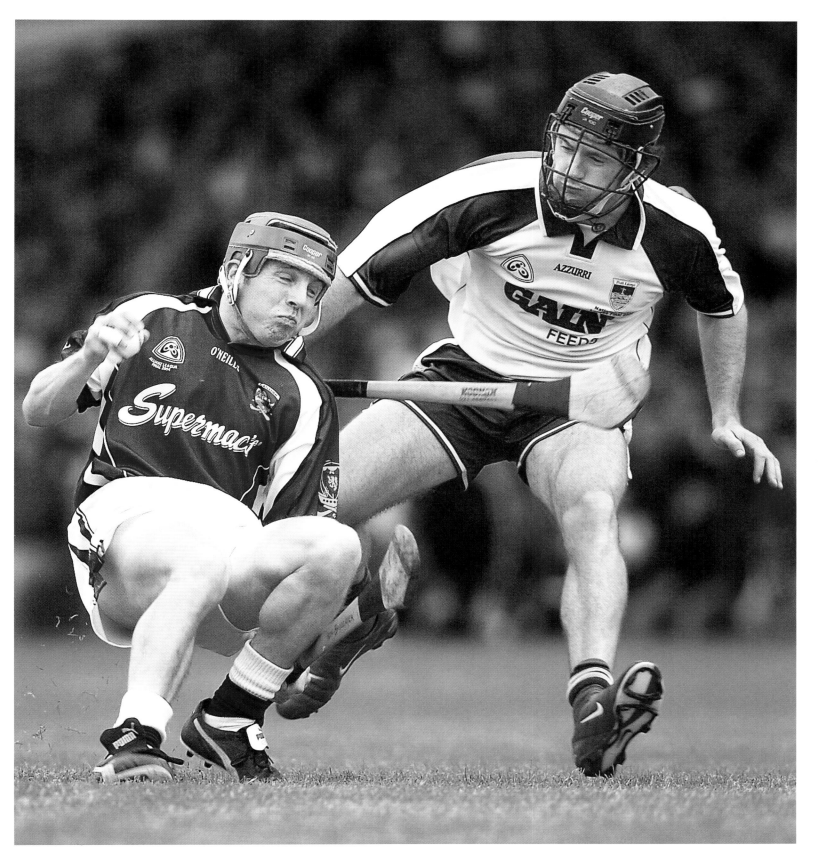

Every summer dawns bright and hopeful for Galway hurling. The National League final with Waterford held out another shimmering mirage of All-Ireland success. Galway won by five points and were worth more. Here, Kevin Broderick loses his footing while James Murray of Waterford muscles in

After the game, Galway manager Conor Hayes stated his belief that Galway had "the two best corner-backs in the country." One of them was their captain Ollie Canning who lifted the trophy on his side's behalf

Bank of Ireland Leinster Football Championship   **Carlow 4-15 Longford 1-16**

The Rebel County? Longford players warming up outside the dressing room area in O'Connor Park, Tullamore, before the championship clash with Carlow

Yeeehar! Three weeks into his job as Carlow manager, Luke Dempsey is riding a winner, as Carlow bump Longford from the Championship with eight points to spare. "In my time as a manager there have been few more satisfying days than today"

Tales from the quiet side. The hurling world doesn't stop when
Kildare and Westmeath come out to play. Nevertheless…
John Shaw of Westmeath gets a hand to the sliotar despite the
interest displayed by David Harney of Kildare

Elevation? Levitation? Ronan Sexton
of Down hovers while Anthony
Gaynor of Cavan chases

The Lone Bannerman of the Apocalypse. Pat Cahill, from Shannon, makes
his way towards Semple Stadium, while the skies are still blue and Clare
still have a chance of winning the Munster title

Some time later… Dan Shanahan, of Waterford, holds up
a finger for each of the three goals he has scored

All-Ireland final 2019???… five year old Laois fan, Jack Reddin, scores
a goal during the half-time break in the Laois versus Meath game at
O'Moore Park, Portlaoise

In Camogie's centenary season, young players represented the foundation for the next
one hundred years. Marie Russell, of Waterford, gets her stroke in despite the keen
attentions of Evelyn Glynn, from Clare, in the Primary Game during the break in the
senior hurling match between the same counties at Semple Stadium

"It's been a burden" said Wexford manager Pat Roe understatedly after Wexford had ended their five year sequence of championship losses. Their win over a surprised Louth side came at Parnell Park where David Devaney of Louth attempts to escape the clutches of John Hegarty from Wexford

Limerick's credentials as football contenders were tested early in the championship game with Tipperary at Páirc Uí Chaoimh. Tipp scored three goals in the opening twenty five minutes before Limerick found the right gear

Bank of Ireland Connacht Football Championship   **Roscommon 1-10 Sligo 0-13**

The Mayor of Maor City addresses the troops about what to do on those days when everyone turns up wearing the same outfit

Frankie Dolan of Roscommon places his face in his hands having failed to place the ball over the bar in the last minute of the game versus Sligo

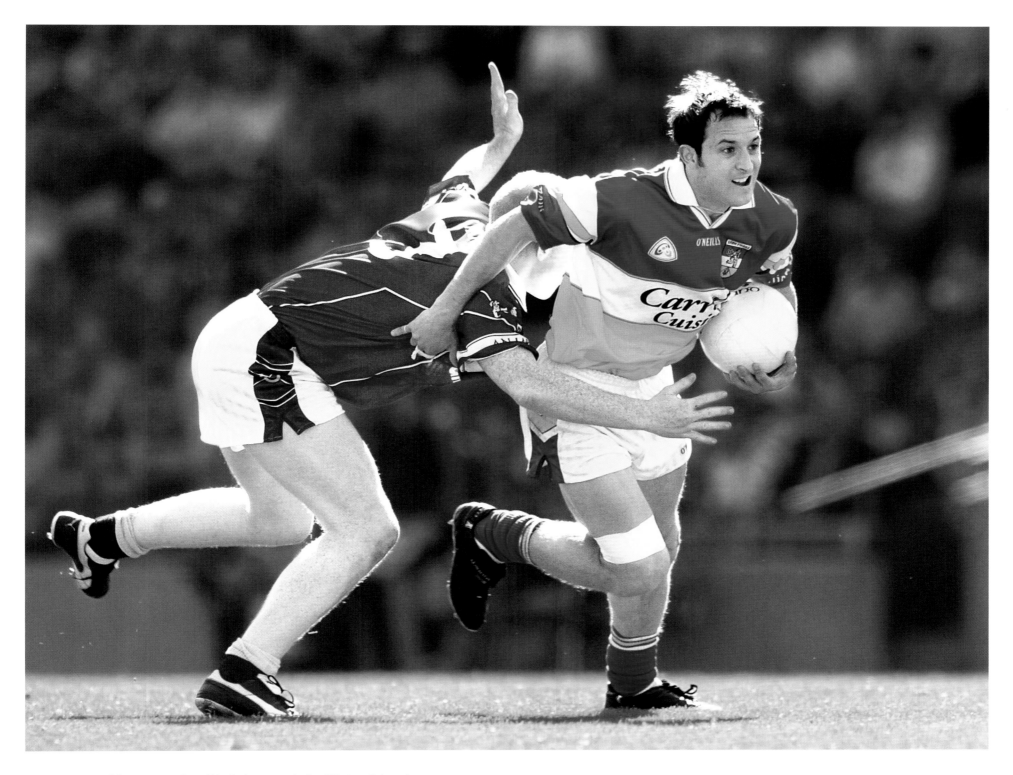

When it was over, Offaly manager Gerry Fahy had to concede that "Westmeath have been waiting a long tme for this day to come." Their patience in the matter of midland derbies was rewarded by instances like Donal O'Donoghue's balanced tackle on Offaly's Roy Malone

During the first half of the game between Clare and Kerry, referee Gerry Kinneavy clashed heads with Clare player Ger Quinlan. With blood flowing freely, Kinneavy had to find a blood sub for himself. Haulie Byrne, who was acting as linesman, was handed the whistle, the cards and the notebook. It would be the second half before Kinneavy would appear again looking like a man who had been in the wars

Armagh 2-19   Monaghan 0-10   Bank of Ireland Ulster Football Championship

Somebody up there doesn't like me. Monaghan manager
Colm Coyle looks to the celestial Ard Comhairle as his
side sink slowly but surely against Armagh

Having being beaten by Monaghan the previous summer,
Armagh's manager Joe Kernan, serenely notes in his diary
that lightning seldom strikes the same place twice

Bank of Ireland Connacht Football Championship   **Sligo 1-15 Roscommon 2-16**

Two slices of Cake. Shane Curran, Roscommon's charismatic goalie, puts a penalty past
his counterpart Phillip Greene of Sligo and then experiences the whole business from
the other side as Paul Taylor drives a penalty into the Roscommon net

May brought a busy weekend to the Whelahan household. Despite being injured, Brian Whelahan brought his customary level of influence to the proceedings as Offaly beat Laois in Tullamore

…And a day later, his father, the legendary Pad Joe Whelahan, has worries of his own.
His Limerick side are close to the end of their game with Cork at the Gaelic Grounds
and close to the end of their Munster championship involvement

Bank of Ireland Leinster Football Championship   **Carlow 1-07   Laois 0-15**

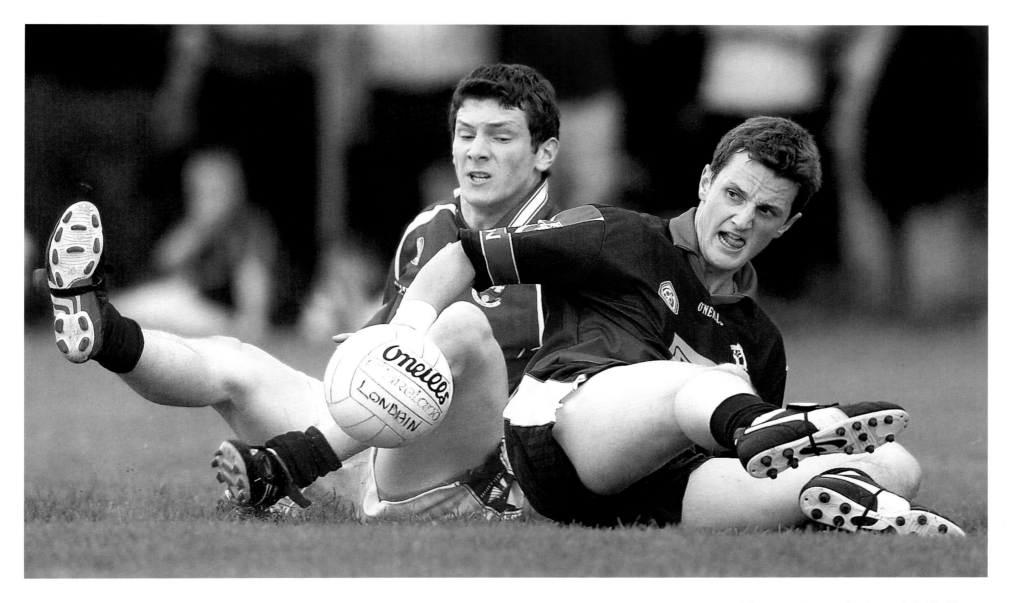

Damien McKenna of London and Michael Meehan of Galway on the seats of their pants in Ruislip. They weren't the only ones. London's involvment in the Connacht Championship has always been moot and being beaten at home by 8-14 to 0-8 in late May rocked them badly

Carlow's summer came to a jarring halt one day on home turf. Laois, still showing signs of the hunger which carried them through 2003, came to town and cut up. Colm Parkinson bursts away from Joe Byrne as Laois keep the dream alive

Bank of Ireland Ulster Football Championship Replay **Cavan 3-13 Down 2-12**

Michael Lyng of Cavan gets the ball away as Sean Farrell of Down comes in to block

Wexford 0-12 Kildare 0-10   Bank of Ireland Leinster Football Championship

Lilywhites into the darkness. It had been eighteen years since Wexford had beaten Kildare in championship football. The sight of it drove the short grass people home to the short grass county

Wexford manager Pat Roe celebrates a modest coup in the company of Sean Quirke, the Wexford county chairman

It's about who you are and where you are from.
John Mullane of Waterford and Michael Herron
of Antrim show the pride

Bank of Ireland Ulster Football Championship   **Tyrone 1-13   Fermanagh 0-12**

Fresh faces into the light. Fermanagh's Shane McDermott leads his team out on to the field for the Ulster championship game against Tyrone

The first hint that Fermanagh had built a team of substance from the debris of winter came in Clones against Tyrone when, despite conceding an early penalty, Charlie Mulgrew's young team, containing six players making their debuts, pushed the All-Ireland champions to the limit. Niall Bogue of Fermanagh and Ciaran Gourley of Tyrone provide a sample of the fare

Bank of Ireland Leinster Football Championship   **Westmeath 0-14   Dublin 0-12**

Dublin's purgatory would be a series of Saturday showdowns with lesser lights.
In June, Ciaran Whelan and his side found themselves grappling with London

For much of the summer Tommy Lyons wore
the persecuted face of a dead man walking.
There were moments though. Beating London
drew the handshake of one wellwisher

Westmeath topple Dublin. The light steps of
Páidí Ó Sé and his selector Jack Cooney tell
the story as eloquently as the closed face of
Tommy Lyons

One for the grandchildren. The Kildare defence on the 12th of June 2004 for the game with Offaly. Enda Murphy,

Michael Foley, Glenn Ryan, Damien Hendy, Eamonn Callaghan, Andrew McLoughlin and Rob McCabe

The game as practised down under. Daniel Hughes of Down and Paul Cashen

discuss which way the water drains from a sink if you are in the antipodes

Bank of Ireland Football Championship Qualifier, Round 1   **Wicklow 1-10 Derry 1-15**

Been there. Seen enough. After his county's defeat to
Derry, Peter Keogh, President of the Wicklow County
Board, picks up his chair and walks

Sprung from the bench. The Cavan side burst into life having had their photo taken

Cavan and Armagh have the sort of history which means that neither takes the other for granted. Brian Mallon of Armagh raises his fists to the skies having scored the final point of the game at Clones

Six children. One Fat Frog pop. The hurling had better be good!

Colm McGuckian of Antrim marks
the winning of another Ulster title

Kerry 0-15   Cork 0-07   Bank of Ireland Munster Football Championship Semi-Final

Fingers stretching into the clouds. Football the old fashioned way. Dermot Hurley of Cork and Darragh Ó Sé of Kerry soar during the Munster semi-final

The summer will end with a Kerry All-Ireland, but, as Cork's Kevin O'Dwyer leaves the pitch in Killarney, he doesn't know that. He thinks that this day is as bad as it will get for a Corkman

Not long before the late late show. Michael Jacob wheels away in celebration having scored Wexford's first goal of a memorable afternoon. At the death his brother Rory will score a second, and hurling's first great shock of the summer will have just occurred

The celebrations to mark liberation. John Conran, the Wexford manager, is embraced by his county chairman Sean Quirke

Sweat and tears. John Hoyne of Kilkenny bears the brunt of a tackle from David "Doc" O'Connor from Wexford

Holder of a famous Leitrim name and holder of the county's promise. Barry Prior celebrates his late point against Roscommon in the Bank of Ireland Connacht Football Championship Semi-Final

In Dublin, it was agreed that the county hurlers "would never have a better chance." Having beaten Offaly convincingly in the League, they perhaps believed it themselves. David Sweeney is an inch or two behind Barry Whelahan of Offaly. So it was for most of the afternoon for the men in blue

Does my bum look big in this? Donegal footballers stand for the
national anthem before their game with Tyrone in Clones

Another McEniff inspired coup. Donegal beat Tyrone.
Brendan Boyle and Damien Diver celebrate

If you could aggregate their experiences you'd
have a tale which stretched to the moon. Sean
Boylan and Mick O'Dwyer shake hands after the
Leinster semi-final. Boylan's face says that Meath
have lost. O'Dwyer's face says that he's been
closer to the summit many times before

Playing against Down out on the Ards Peninsula is always a little different. The environment where hurling
isn't uniformly welcome and the crossing of the Lough on the Strangford ferry make the experience
unique. Conor Hayes, the Galway manager, enjoys the voyage

Shane Curran marches to the beat of a different drum

Guinness Hurling Championship Qualifier, Round 1   **Clare 7-19 Laois 2-15**

…and Donie Ryan of Limerick is broken and bowed by the sound of the final whistle against Tipperary

Bad days, bad times. Warm afternoons, hot tears. Paul Cuddy
of Laois as his sides game with Clare draws to an end

In the era of e-Commerce, some business executives still favour the approach of direct selling

Citizens of the People's Republic of Cork stage a mass gathering at the Munster Hurling Final. Not a leopard skin hat among them

When Páidí Ó Sé bounced into Westmeath on the rebound, having been jilted by his beloved
Kerry, he could hardly have expected days like these. Páidí and Dessie Dolan celebrate
Westmeath's progress to a Leinster final

Once in a blue moon. Ken McGrath is held aloft in the centre of
a sea of his countyfolk as Waterford celebrate one of the great
days. In his turn, McGrath holds the Munster trophy on high

Some times neighbourly feuds are just feral and desperate. Galway and Mayo have known each other too long for it to be any other way. Conor Moran bursts with the ball. Tommy Joyce stretches every muscle as he gives chase

"If we can't get it going in half an hour just tell me what you want to say. And it had better not be a comment about the weather"

Referee Jimmy McKee has his earpiece adjusted by linesman Con Costello late in the game between Longford and Waterford

Jimmy mc Kee.

JULY 3

Bank of Ireland Football Championship Qualifier, Round 2   **Leitrim 0-04 Dublin 1-13**

Halfway through the highways and by-ways tour and Tommy Lyons is in Leitrim. The rain is getting underneath his collar. The football is poor. Where did all the good times go?

98

A SEASON OF SUNDAYS 2004

All summer Sean Cavanagh of Tyrone was just about unstoppable. Martin Cole of Down joins the list of those who have suffered at his hands

Bank of Ireland Football Championship Qualifier, Round 2 **Fermanagh 0-19 Meath 2-12**

Perhaps Meath knew that they'd reached an impasse in their progress when they were defeated by Fermanagh for the second summer in succession. It would be sometime before Fermanagh's displays showed that there was no shame in losing to them. Joe Sheridan's radar is a little off as Fermanagh's Declan O'Reilly gains possession in Enniskillen

Colm Bradley celebrates Fermanagh's progress with one of the sides selectors

An epic afternoon at Celtic Park. Extra time needed to take Derry and Cavan out of their clinch. Twelve yellow cards flashed. And Paddy Bradley's four points in injury time, one of the main instruments of Cavan's demise. Bradley leans back as others lean forward. Here, Anthony Forde attempts the block

Love the coat, did they have it in any other colour? Brian Whelahan of Offaly has a word with President Mary McAleese while Gary Hanniffy plays gooseberry

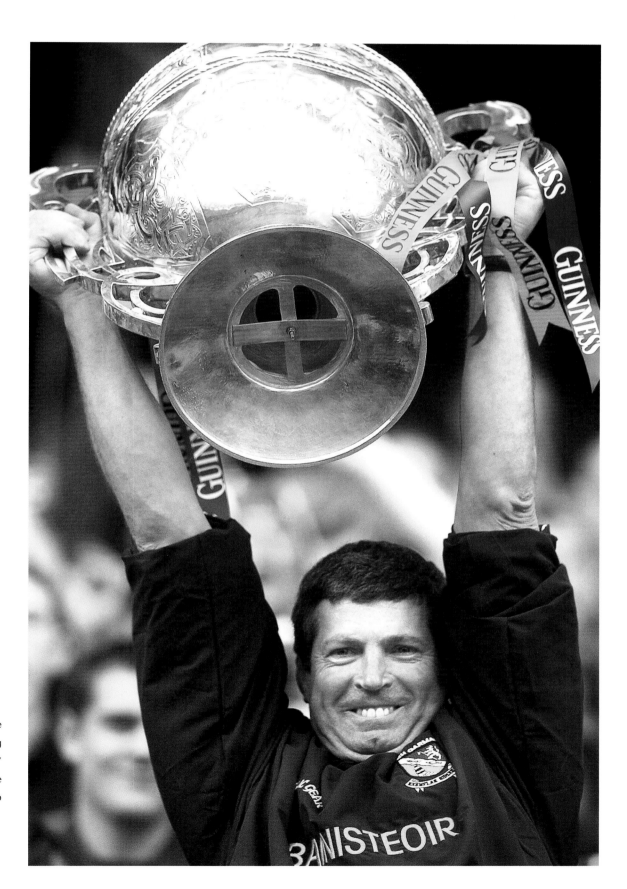

"Experience is a great thing," said John Conran, "we've
been at the wrong side of Leinster finals for a long
number of years. Offaly have been killers for us."
Today though, Wexford survive. Conran gets to lift the
Bob O'Keeffe Cup

On an afternoon in July, the hurlers of Tipperary and Cork travelled to Killarney to fight for their lives. Both sides had been bounced out of the Munster championship. Both knew that the losers would have to rebuild painfully. Tipp had never been beaten in Killarney. Cork had lost an agonising Munster final. It was one of those days when heroes are made and Niall McCarthy gave us a glimpse of the shape of his wonderful year by scoring 1-2 and submitting an immense performance

When Alan Brogan returned from Australia in the spring, things began to look up for Dublin. It got a little better when Ian Robertson returned from the injury plagued wilderness he had been in. Dublin's best showing of the summer came in Portlaoise one evening against Longford. Brogan and Robertson celebrate the latters' goal

Bank of Ireland Ulster Football Championship Final   **Armagh 3-15 Donegal 0-11**

Anticipating a clash between Tyrone and Armagh, the All-Ireland champions of the previous two summers, the Ulster Council rented a bigger hall for their showpiece match. Tyrone never made it to Croke Park but the unflickering optimism of Donegal people was enough to draw a crowd of 67,136 paying customers to see Armagh play some of the sweetest football of the year

Armagh rattled three into the Donegal net. Paddy McKeever celebrates scoring the first

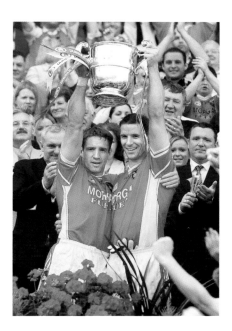

Kieran McGeeney and Paul McGrane lift the Ulster trophy

Bank of Ireland Munster Football Championship Final   **Limerick 1-10   Kerry 1-10**

It was a day when Limerick tried to win the Munster title and then tried to lose it. Kerry never led in the second half but Limerick lacked the self belief to go and close the deal. 108 years and waiting for a while longer as Johnny Murphy and John Quane, hidden, contest a high ball with Darragh Ó Sé

If Kilkenny were to have another bad day we assumed it might be against Galway who had laid out such elaborate tripwires back in 2001. As it happened, Kilkenny were irresistible on that evening in Semple Stadium. Eddie Brennan celebrates scoring his sides third goal in the most impressive demonstration of power hurling which the champions offered this year

JULY *17*   Bank of Ireland Football Championship Qualifier, Round 3   **Fermangh 0-18 Cork 0-12**

After Fermanagh waltzed to victory over Cork, Liam McBarron had a quick shower, hugged Father Brian D'Arcy and boarded a helicopter for Kinawley in Fermanagh where he got married. Quote of the day belonged to Ger Canning, "Can Liam McBarron score on his wedding day? And I mean on the field of play."

When Tyrone met Galway something more than the end of the season was going to greet the losers. A small congregation one Saturday afternoon witnessed the last rites for the John O'Mahony era in Galway. Brian McGuigan of Tyrone, seen here with head bowed low, scored the only goal of a dour game. Paul Clancy of Galway fights on

JULY *17*   Guinness Hurling Championship Qualifier, Round 3   **Clare 3-16 Offaly 2-10**

Hats on. Feet up. Two spectators discussing the form in the Gaelic Grounds

A bumper year for the Connacht Council. Attendances in the province were up 74% on last season. Even allowing for two lucrative replays attendances still rose by 36%. On the day of the provincial final 34,790 shoehorned themselves into McHale Park in Castlebar to see Mayo and Roscommon in action

The best day of Mayo's summer and the cup shows it's face to the faithful. Mayo captain Fergal Costello lifts the Nestor Cup after his side's win over Roscommon in the Bank of Ireland Connacht Senior Football Championship Final

Bank of Ireland Munster Football Championship Final Replay   **Kerry 3-10   Limerick 2-09**

In the replayed Munster Football final, Limerick knocked Kerry to the canvas with a goal after fifteen seconds, but, in front of a home crowd in Killarney, Kerry recovered. Darragh Ó Sé and Jason Stokes keep their eyes on the prize

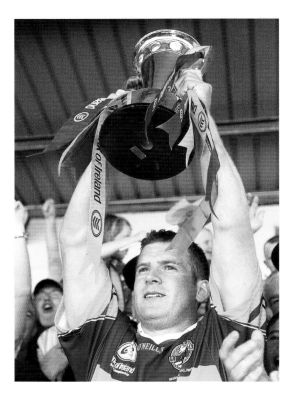

Dara Ó Cinnéide lifts the Munster trophy

Laois and Westmeath would need two meetings to separate them also. Brian Morley of Westmeath and Padraig Clancy of Laois both get a hand to the ball

Having been suspended in an earlier match, Westmeath midfielder Rory O'Connell won an interlocutory injunction in the High Court allowing him to play in the Leinster final. After twenty minutes he is introduced to the action replacing Gary Dolan in midfield

Bank of Ireland Leinster Football Championship Final **Westmeath 0-13 Laois 0-13**

The Master and his graduate pupil both grown silver haired. Páidí and Micko shake hands at the end of the drawn Leinster final

Fermanagh's magical mystery tour rolls on and on. Eamon Maguire, scorer of his team's only goal
against Donegal in the 4th round qualifier, celebrates with team captain Shane McDermott

"They just needed to be tidied up a little." So said Páidí O Sé of his charges in Westmeath when he had tidied and brought them to an historic Leinster title. Captain David O'Shaughnessy lifts the Leinster trophy

Páidí and his co-conspirator from Kerry, Tomás O Flaharta, celebrate on the Croke Park turf

Cork seldom had to show their full hand while getting past Antrim in the All-Ireland quarter-final. Niall McCarthy played like a high roller all season however. Tackled by Antrim's Michael McCambridge, he retains all the aces

Impressionable young men. Tommy Walsh of Kilkenny tussles with Niall Gilligan of Clare in the drawn match between their counties in Croke Park. Gilligan is in the helmet. Walsh is bare headed

One week later. Tommy Walsh of Kilkenny tussles with Niall Gilligan of Clare in the replayed match between their counties in Semple Stadium. This week, Walsh wears the helmet and Gilligan goes bare headed

Bank of Ireland All-Ireland Football Championship, Round 4   **Dublin 1-14   Roscommon 0-13**

The index of success 1.
Jason Sherlock points skywards having
goaled for Dublin in the 4th round qualifier
against Roscommon in Croke Park

The index of success 2.
Eoin Mulligan points to team-mate Sean
Cavanagh having scored his side's opening
goal in the 4th round qualifier against Laois

Bank of Ireland All-Ireland Football Championship Quarter-Final   **Fermanagh 0-12   Armagh 0-11**

On and on, Fermanagh's great odyssey of a summer
continues and Colm Bradley leaps to celebrate the
latest claimed scalp, that of Armagh

Mayo teams in Croke Park are never entirely to be trusted. Often they travel in confidence, go home without hope. This year looked to be different though, when they outplayed the All-Ireland champions Tyrone in the All-Ireland quarter-final

Waterford's summer had a peak and a descent. Following the happy glory of the Munster final against Cork, they had to wait and wait for their crack at Kilkenny. Too long waiting perhaps. Kilkenny had become acclimatised to the Championship again. James Murray feels the pain of a bumpy landing

Through many toils, dangers and fears, have they already come. Brian Cody and DJ Carey embrace as Kilkenny, after a summer of turbulence, reach the All-Ireland final and give life to the dream of three in a row

James Donagy of Derry hitches a ride on the back of Fergal Wilson of Westmeath. Derek Heavin, to the left, does the can-can in celebration

Summer training. Dublin are playing Kerry and a train driver stops his locomotive to peer into the game

Blues snooze. The inevitability of Kerry's continued dominance over Dublin gets to Niamh Finnegan of Finglas as the two counties play out their All-Ireland quarter-final appearance

The moment when Dublin's season turned and died. Dara Ó Cinnéide bears down on the sky blue goal. Stephen Cluxton advances gamely.

Ó Cinnéide has already purchased all the time he needs however. He shoots, he scores. Dublin never fully recover

Guinness All-Ireland Hurling Championship Semi-Final   **Cork 1-27 Wexford 0-12**

The pleasures of being a mature student. Before Fermanagh's semi-final with Mayo, Hugh Murray, of Roslea, reads his programme and hopes that his countymen are as well prepared for the elements as he is

Behind every great man. Cork manager Donal O'Grady celebrates with his mother Kitty after his team's easy victory over Wexford in the All-Ireland hurling semi-final

Bank of Ireland Football Championship Semi-Final Replay   **Mayo 0-13   Fermanagh 1-08**

Bleached blinder. Conor Mortimer of Mayo clenches the fist and lets out a roar of joy after scoring a late point against Fermanagh

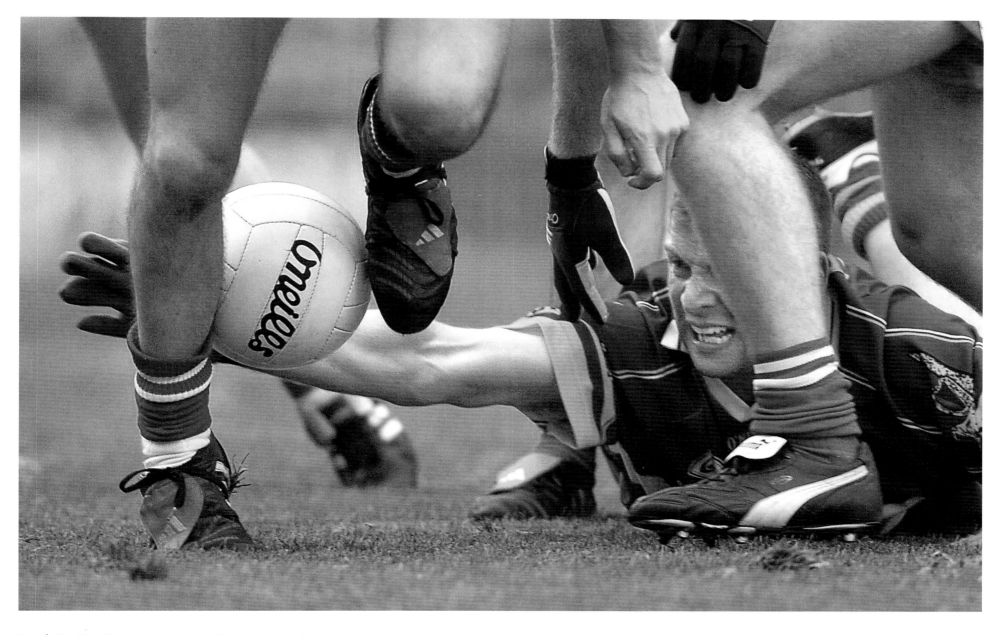

Dara Ó Cinnéide of Kerry makes a flat out effort to get possession amidst a thicket of Derry legs in the All-Ireland football semi-final

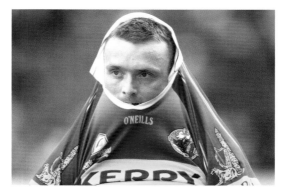

Paddy Bradley unenthusiastically slips into the jersey of his team's conquerors

All-Ireland Minor Hurling Championship Final   **Galway 3-12 Kilkenny 1-18**

The minor hurling final between Galway and Kilkenny turned out to be a classic in two installments. Kevin Hynes of Galway scoots clear of Kilkenny's Ronan Maher in the drawn game

Hello to the Hill. Perfectly orderered earlycomers to the All-Ireland hurling final
take their positions on the fresh concrete of the new Hill 16

Himself, he said nothing, but many came to Croke Park on All-Ireland final day imagining it would be their last chance to see

DJ Carey in the Kilkenny colours. DJ produced many of the moments that would make such a pilgrimage worthwhile,

accelerating away here from the attentions of John Gardiner and Ben O'Connor

Over the space of two seasons, Tommy Walsh, of Tullaroan and Kilkenny, has emerged as a player who electrifies the crowd every time he gets

the ball into his hand. Leaving Timmy McCarthy behind him and Niall McCarthy on the deck, he gives a sample of just why that is so

Most people's hurler of the year
in full flight. Seán Óg Ó hAilpín
in a typically athletic moment

Old comrades Brian Corcoran and
Joe Deane come together to
celebrate another All-Ireland win

The red sea. Cork rebirth as a hurling power has opened up the joy of the game to a new generation

In March, Ben O'Connor came to Croke Park and won
a club All-Ireland with Newtownshandrum. Six months
later, he was back again, this time to personally hoist
the Liam MacCarthy Cup. All in all a good year

All-Ireland Minor Hurling Championship Final Replay   **Galway 0-16   Kilkenny 1-12**

Galway and Kilkenny had to do it all again in the minor final. Richie Hogan, cousin of DJ and burdened with all that goes with that, loses out here to David Kennedy of Galway

Like their senior counterparts, the Kilkenny minors were striving for a third All-Ireland win in a row.

Gavin Nolan learns that those finals are tough ones to lose

In 2003, John Lee was on the Galway team which lost to Kilkenny by just a point in the All-Ireland minor final. In 2004, it took a replay to separate the teams but Lee was still at centre-back and this time, as captain, he lifted the silver

Fionnuala Carr, the daughter of former Down All-Ireland medal winner Ross Carr, chases the sliotar while Mairead
Holland, Elizabeth Bugler and Valerie O'Sullivan chase her in the All-Ireland junior camogie final

More silver deposited at the banks of the Lee.
Valerie O'Keeffe celebrates the winning of the
All-Ireland junior camogie final

Emer Dillon bursts through the Tipperary defence in the All-Ireland senior camogie final. Sinead Nealon has just two ends of a broken stick with which to stop her

"C'mon Drom n' Inch" roared Joanne Ryan just before lifting the O'Duffy Cup. After decades of famine, Tipperary had just won the title for the fifth time in six seasons

The Gaynor dynasty in which Len's haul of three All-Ireland medals seems ever more paltry when set against the collection amassed by his daughter Ciara

Tyrone 0-12   Kerry 0-10   All-Ireland Minor Football Championship Final

The pain starts here. The minors of Kerry and Tyrone were prepared to cross lines and ship hard knocks in pursuit of a future

Tyrone captain Marc Cunningham lifts the minor trophy bringing underage glory to his county for the second time in six years

His counterpart Shane Murphy of Kerry counts the cost

Bank of Ireland All-Ireland Football Championship Final   **Kerry 1-20   Mayo 2-09**

Marching to their own rhythm, marching to their downfall. Mayo footballers turn a corner in Croke Park on All-Ireland day

Five minutes into the All-Ireland final and Trevor Mortimer harasses Michael McCarthy until he loses the ball. Mortimer lofts a pass
to Alan Dillon, who coolly sidesteps Kerry goalie Diarmuid Murphy and shoots a goal for Mayo

Bank of Ireland All-Ireland Football Championship Final   **Kerry 1-20   Mayo 2-09**

There's a thin line between winning and losing. Usually. The furrowed brows belong to Mayo people, the rampant flags are those of The Kingdom. Guess who's winning?

"Maurice (Fitzgerald) in his day had it all and Colm is so young, I haven't seen a guy with as much natural skill since. The goal, the dummy he gave just before he kicked it, was incredible. He gave an exhibition."
Seamus Moynihan on Colm 'The Gooch' Cooper

As the All-Ireland football final wore on, Mayo's
Kieran McDonald was forced to drop further
and further back. Here, he does the chasing on
Kerry forward Liam Hassett

SEPTEMBER *26*

"The hunger was a thing you couldn't quantify" said Jack O'Connor afterwards.

Something about the response to victory gave an indication of how famished Kerry were. Colm Cooper is hoisted aloft by team-mates and Jack O'Connor is embraced by county chairman Sean Walsh

Bank of Ireland All-Ireland Football Championship Final   **Kerry 1-20 Mayo 2-09**

All's well that ends well. After a season long struggle with injury, Seamus Moynihan, the Kerry talisman, got to enjoy the luxury of entering the All-Ireland final when the game was all but won. Standing on the steps of the Hogan Stand a little while later, made all the lonely days of physio worthwhile

Bathed in flashlights, the cup glinting in the September air and about to make a passionate speech in his native Irish, Dara Ó Cinnéide reaches the summit for any player and lifts the Sam Maguire

And below on the pitch, Kieran McDonald, who helped drag Mayo to this place, absorbs the pain of falling at the last hurdle

The Jackies of Dublin came to Croke Park for the second successive September and found that their luck against western opposition hadn't improved. Dublin had the jitters. Galway had the class. Ashling McCormack, of Dublin, reaches with Ann-Marie McDonagh of Galway during the TG4 Ladies Senior All-Ireland Football Final

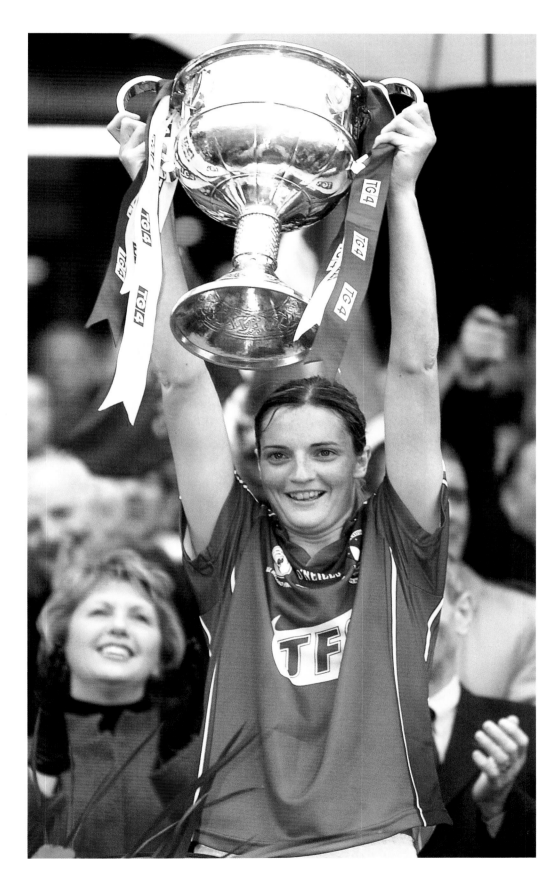

The first time is always the sweetest. Annette Clarke becomes the first ever Galway captain to lift the Brendan Martin Cup

Losing is such sweet sorrow. Ashling McCormack, of Dublin, pensively watches her team's conquerors climb the steps of the Hogan Stand at the end of the All-Ireland final

Coca-Cola International Rules Series   **Ireland 3-17-08 (77)   Australia 1-09-08 (41)**

He ain't heavy, he's my brother. As the Irish side stand together during the national anthems preceding the first test between
Ireland and Australia, Setanta Ó hAilpín, the exiled god of hurling, rests an arm on the shoulder of his brother Seán Óg

Blowing away the past. Saxophone player Rebecca Cradden, a member of the Artane Band, plays before the first test between Ireland and Australia. The occasion marked the first time that girls have played with the band in Croke Park

Round ball game. Dean Solomon, left, and Andrew Embley of Australia, attempt to get to grips with the new shape of ball and a new shape of opponent,

Seán Óg Ó hAilpín, and Martin McGrath, hidden, of Ireland, during the first test of the Coca-Cola International Rules Series 2004

Down and out from down under. Dejected and surprised Australian fans sit in the stand and reflect after the first test between Ireland and Australia. Ireland won by thirty six points, effectively killing the series

Coca-Cola International Rules Series   **Ireland 1-13-10 (55)   Australia 0-13-02 (41)**

The last lifting job of a long season. Padraig Joyce, captain of Ireland, hoists the Cormac McAnallen Cup to mark Ireland's win

Every underdog has his day. David Heaney of Ireland holds onto the leather as Max Hudghton of Australia gets ready for an emergency landing during the second test at Croke Park